CROAK

A book of fun for frog lovers

Compiled by Professor Phil Bishop

EXISLE
PUBLISHING

Introduction

Everyone can recognize frogs and from a very early age most of us develop a love and fascination for them. Children love frogs and toads, and like me, many of us never grow out of this. They are found on every continent (except Antarctica); they appear in fairytales, folklore, songs and are part of many cultures … but what is a frog?

Toads, bullfrogs and treefrogs are simply different kinds of frogs which belong to a group of animals called Amphibians. While many people may think that frogs are either green or brown, they come in every different colour and hue from red to blue. Most amphibians are long-lived with some reaching the grand old age of 45 years in the wild. They have been on this earth for millions of years and were hopping around the feet of the dinosaurs.

Most frogs lead a double life, where they lay their eggs in water, which then turn into tadpoles and later metamorphose into miniature adults, with a tail that is quickly absorbed.

However, there are many that don't do this — some sit over their eggs and guard them, some lay their eggs above ground, others carry tadpoles around on their back, and still others give birth to live young, either as tadpoles or baby frogs that they incubated in their stomachs.

Although we discover several new species of frogs each week, they are disappearing much faster than any other group of land animals, with more than 40 per cent of all species facing extinction. We need to look after the frogs now more than ever, otherwise our children, and their children, will never feel the enchantment of holding one of these beautiful creatures in their own hands and gazing into its very wise and ancient eyes. I have devoted my life to studying frogs and will not stop trying to save them from extinction until the day I die.

As I'm sure you'll see in this book, frogs are truly beautiful, extraordinary and amazing animals. For more information on each frog pictured, please refer to pages 158–159.

I have always loved frogs
and toads — a love probably
triggered by Jeremy Fisher.

JANE GOODALL

Look deep into nature, and then you will understand everything better.

ALBERT EINSTEIN

We should be working
really hard to save the frogs
— like our lives depend on
them … because they do!

PHIL BISHOP

I have heard tree frogs in an orchestration as complicated as Bach singing in a forest lit by a million emerald fireflies.

GERALD DURRELL

I taught myself how to write and draw comics at a young age. Possibly under the influence of toad venom.

IAN WILSON

Actor, conservationist,
friend of frogs.

HARRISON FORD

Amphibians — the word comes from the Greek meaning 'double life'.

ELIZABETH KOLBERT

CROAK

17

I'd kiss a frog even if there was no promise of a Prince Charming popping out of it. I love frogs.

CAMERON DIAZ

Amphibians are found almost all over the world. They even live in oases or sand dunes, which are probably the last places you'd expect.

SIMON STUART

The toad, without which no garden would be complete.

CHARLES DUDLEY WARNER

More fun than a frog

in a glass of milk.

BOB WEIR

Theories pass. The frog remains.

JEAN ROSTAND

As a herpetologist, I have many friends in low places.

NEVILLE PASSMORE

The sound of your croaky voice
is but sweet music to my ears.

ARIADNE ANGULO

The frog forgets that
he was once a tadpole.

KOREAN PROVERB

It wasn't a kiss that changed the
frog, but the fact that a young girl
looked beneath warts and slime and
believed she saw a prince.

RICHELLE E. GOODRICH

Arm yourself when the
Frog God smiles.

FRANK HERBERT

Although conservation must
be scientifically grounded, it is
actually a moral issue of beauty,
ethics, and spiritual values.

GEORGE SCHALLER

Sometimes you never know
the true value of a creature,
until it becomes a memory.

SUZY CATO

Ask a toad what is beauty; he
will answer that it is a female
with two great round eyes
coming out of her little head,
a large flat mouth, a yellow
belly and a brown back.

VOLTAIRE

I have loved being involved
with the amazing world of frogs
for many years and I hope that
our children and grandchildren
learn to value and appreciate this
fascinating group of animals.

DEBBIE BISHOP

If we can discover the meaning
in the trilling of a frog, perhaps
we may understand why it is for
us not merely noise but a song of
poetry and emotion.

ADRIAN FORSYTH

This is, I believe, the first instance known of a 'flying frog'.

ALFRED RUSSEL WALLACE

It is a privilege to be conscious
in the Universe, to live on this
particular planet, and to share it
with so many goodly creatures.
We can destroy them easily
enough but with somewhat
greater effort we could save
them, just as we save ourselves.

COLIN TUDGE

I think I've kissed a prince ...
I hope he doesn't turn into a frog.

E.L. JAMES

Above all, watch with glittering eyes the whole world around, because the greatest secrets are always hidden in the most unlikely places.

ROALD DAHL

There is no place in a city that can't be better. There is no toad that can't be a princess, no frog that can't become a prince.

JAIME LERNER

I have four dogs, four horses, a cat, and a bunch of wild frogs.

DARYL HANNAH

I'm in love with a big, blue frog.

PETER, PAUL AND MARY

Truly spectacular natural history exists among amphibians — go to the tropics and you will never cease to be amazed by the marvel of amphibian nature!

JOS KIELGAST

Frogs have it made; they
get to eat what bugs them.

ANONYMOUS

Every little frog is great
in his own bog.

IRISH PROVERB

You can't tell by the look of a
frog how far they'll jump.

PAUL DOIRON

Curb your fretting, tadpole,
or the frog of your future
will fail to croak.

PAUL COLLINS

I went into a French restaurant
and asked the waiter,
'Have you got frog's legs?'
He said, 'Yes,' so I said,
'Well hop into the kitchen and
get me a cheese sandwich.'

TOMMY COOPER

There are not frogs
wherever there is water; but
wherever there are frogs
water will be found.

GOETHE

A toad dressed in three shades of brown,
came in from a night on the town.
He paused by my shoe, to deposit a poo,
Then climbed in and settled right down.

LES MINTER

On damp nights the chorus of frogs and toads which swarm in weedy backyards creates such a bewildering uproar that it is impossible to carry on a conversation indoors except by shouting.

JAMES ORTON

Frog in the mud is happier
than the man, because it has no
ambition to reach the stars!

MEHMET MURAT ILDAN

If it's your job to eat a frog, it's best to do it first thing in the morning.

MARK TWAIN

Sweet are the uses of adversity which, like the toad, ugly and venomous, wears yet a precious jewel in his head.

WILLIAM SHAKESPEARE

When we save the frogs,
we're protecting all our
wildlife, all our ecosystems
and all humans.

KERRY KRIGER

It wouldn't be at all difficult
for me to kiss a woman — I'll
kiss a frog if you like.

STEPHEN FRY

Comedian, cyclist,
frog-translator.

ROBIN WILLIAMS

He has no faith in principles,
only in frogs.

IVAN TURGENEV

Frogs with dirty little lips.

FRANK ZAPPA

If frogs could fly — well,
we'd still be in this mess, but
wouldn't it be neat?

DREW CAREY

I look like a tree toad who
was changed into a boy but
not completely.

GARRISON KEILLOR

The conservation of biodiversity
starts on our plate.

GONÇALO M. ROSA

Frogs are more often heard
than seen. Their voices remind
us of the need for dialogue,
which begins by listening.

ULMAR GRAFE

The frog knows more about
the rain than the calendar.

CREOLE PROVERB

The things I do for frogs!

PRINCE CHARLES

My Fiat Multipla is bright green
— it looks like a frog. I look like a
monkey, so between the two of us,
we are a hideous prospect.

DOMINIC HOLLAND

Every child should have mud pies, grasshoppers, water bugs, tadpoles, frogs, mud turtles, elderberries, wild strawberries, acorns, chestnuts, trees to climb.

LUTHER BURBANK

We think too small, like the frog at the bottom of the well. He thinks the sky is only as big as the top of the well. If he surfaced, he would have an entirely different view.

MAO ZEDONG

Time's fun when you're
having flies.

KERMIT THE FROG

I think most people don't realize that little creatures like frogs can live so long. I certainly didn't.

JANE GOODALL

Seeing the tiny heart of a tadpole beating made me feel like I should care, even if I'm the only one.

AMAËL BORZÉE

Though they include some of the world's noisiest, most colourful, and most poisonous animals, frogs are typically shy and retiring creatures, rarely encountered by humans.

TIM HALLIDAY

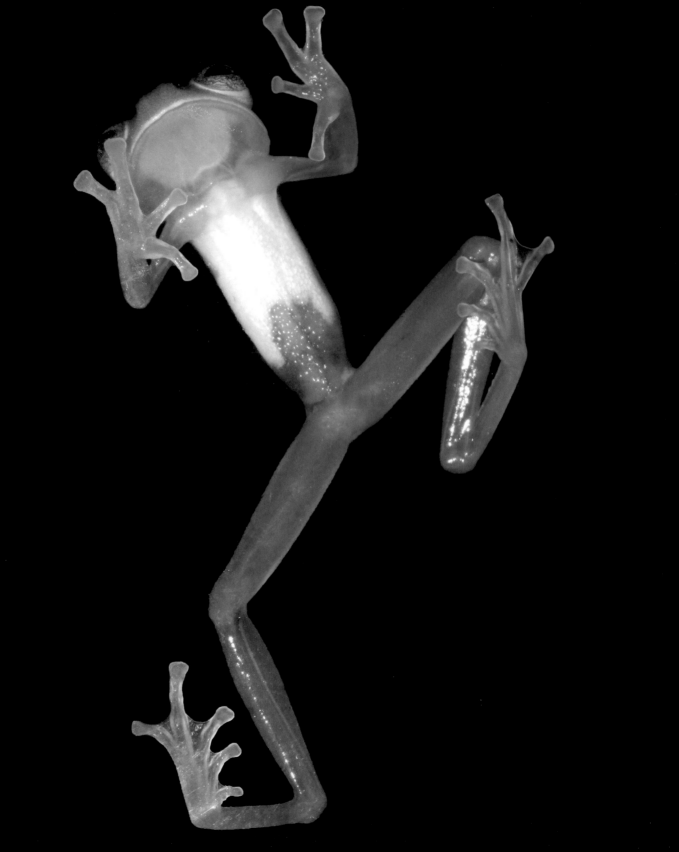

It would be quite interesting
to use Kermit the Frog
to act like a real frog.
But it wouldn't produce
captivating theatre.

MARIANNE ELLIOTT

Every frog has his day.

LOU REED

If we act now to save frogs then our children's children might be able to hear the sound of a healthy planet.

JODI ROWLEY

The golden toad was the
first documented victim of
global warming.

TIM FLANNERY

Listening to a chorus of frogs
helps me to connect to nature
in a deep and magical way.

KATHERINE KENNARD

That's why my green is feeling grey
Sometimes even frogs have rainy days.

KERMIT THE FROG

The amphibian is … in many respects, little more than a peculiar type of fish which is capable of walking on land.

ALFRED SHERWOOD ROMER

I can look like a frog.

KATY PERRY

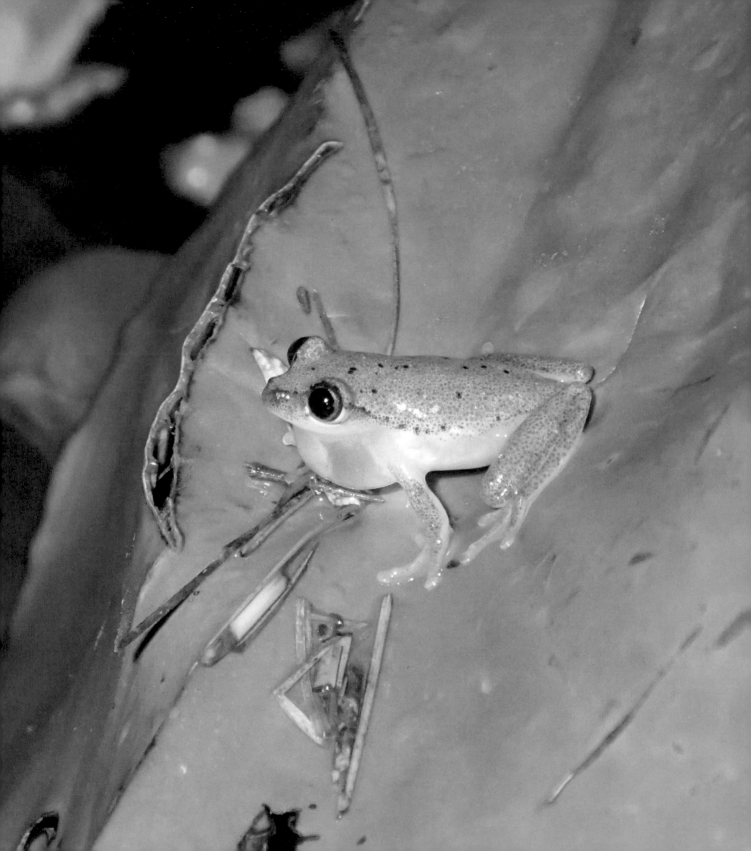

The sound, which the scientific books describe as 'croaking', floats far and wide, and produces a beautiful, mysterious effect on a still evening.

WILLIAM HENRY HUDSON

Frogs tragically are vanishing.

JEAN-MICHEL COUSTEAU

Many scientists claim that amphibians are important bioindicators — a sort of barometer of Earth's health, since they are more sensitive to environmental stress than other organisms.

ASHLEY MATTOON

If we really care for
ourselves we will care for
all of the rest of the world.

GEORGE RABB

If you want to achieve conservation, the first thing you have to do is persuade people that the natural world is precious, beautiful, worth saving and complex.

DAVID ATTENBOROUGH

That is the way it is done, the way it has always been done. Frogs have every right to expect it will always be done that way.

JOHN STEINBECK

Be kind and tender to the Frog;
And do not call him names,
as 'Slimy skin' or 'Polly-wog';
Or likewise 'Ugly James'.

HILAIRE BELLOC

How many beers do y'all think
it takes before one international
scientist turns to another and says,
'Dude, bet you twenty bucks I can
levitate a frog with a magnet?'

ROBYN SCHNEIDER

I have been told that while all frogs begin their lives as tadpoles, not all tadpoles become frogs.

ROBERT POGUE HARRISON

When the Moon is
moved by a choir of
frogs, it rains at night.

LUIS F. MARIN DA FONTE

Information about photographs

For more information about these frogs and frog conservation please visit these websites:
www.amphibians.org,
www.iucn-amphibians.org,
www.amphibiaweb.org,
www.nzfrogs.org.

Page no.	Species name and location	Photographer
1	*Ranoidea wilcoxii* (Australia)	Phil Bishop
2	*Megaphrys nasuta* (Borneo)	Phil Bishop
4	*Boophis elenae* (Madagascar)	Gonçalo M. Rosa
6	*Limnonectes khulii* (Borneo, Brunei)	Debbie Bishop
8	*Megophrys nasuta* (Borneo, Brunei)	Phil Bishop
10	*Philautus acutus* (Borneo)	Ulmar Grafe
12	*Prynoidis juxtasper* (Borneo, Brunei)	Phil Bishop
14	*Boana faber* (Brazil)	Luis F. Marin da Fonte
16	*Andinobates minutus* (Panama)	Gonçalo M. Rosa
18	*Melanophryniscus admirabilis* (Brazil)	Luis F. Marin da Fonte
20	*Notaden bennettii* (Australia)	Phil Bishop
22	*Ingerophrynus divergens* (Borneo, Sarawak)	Phil Bishop
24	*Heterixalus madagascariensis* (Madagascar)	Debbie Bishop
26	*Hylarana luctuosa* (Borneo)	Ulmar Grafe
28	*Kassina senegalensis* (Africa)	Jos Kielgast
30	*Atelopus spumarius* (Peru)	Ariadne Angulo
32	*Microhyla borneensis* (Borneo, Sarawak)	Debbie Bishop
34	*Rhinella marina* (Australia)	Phil Bishop
36	*Ceratophrys cranwelli* (Argentina)	Debbie Bishop
38	*Ansonia latidisca* (Borneo, Sarawak)	Phil Bishop
40	*Leiopelma archeyi* (New Zealand)	James Reardon
42	*Atelopus zeteki* (Pananma)	Gonçalo M. Rosa
44	*Bufo bufo* (England)	Phil Bishop
46	*Boana guentheri* (Argentina)	Phil Bishop
48	*Rhacophorus nigropalmatus* (Borneo, Brunei)	Phil Bishop
50	*Hylarana raniceps* (Borneo, Brunei)	Phil Bishop
52	*Nannophrys marmorata* (Sri Lanka)	James Reardon
54	*Osteocephalus taurinus* (Peru)	Ariadne Angulo
56	*Rentapia hosii* (Borneo, Brunei)	Phil Bishop
58	*Breviceps gibbosus* (South Africa)	Les Minter
60	*Oophaga vicentei* (Panama)	Gonçalo M. Rosa
62	*Hemisus marmoratus* (Africa)	Jos Kielgast
64	*Philautus schmarda* (Sri Lanka)	James Reardon
66	*Ranoidea raniformis* (New Zealand)	Debbie Bishop
68	*Staurois guttatus* (Borneo, Brunei)	Phil Bishop
70	*Staurois guttatus* metamorph (Borneo, Brunei)	Ulmar Grafe
72	*Polypedates otilophus* (Borneo, Brunei)	Phil Bishop
74	*Limnonectes leporinus* (Borneo, Brunei)	Phil Bishop
76	*Breviceps gibbosus* (South Africa)	Les Minter
78	*Ranoidea chloris* (Australia)	Phil Bishop
80	*Telmatobufo bullocki* (Chile)	Phil Bishop
82	*Agalychnis lemur* (Panama)	Gonçalo M. Rosa
84	*Prynoidis juxtasper* (Borneo, Brunei)	Phil Bishop

86	*Ranoidea wilcoxii* (Australia)	Phil Bishop
88	*Dyscophus antongilii* (Madagascar)	Phil Bishop
90	*Centrolenidae* — Glass frog (Peru)	Ariadne Angulo
92	*Polypedates otilophus* (Borneo, Sarawak)	Debbie Bishop
94	*Oreophrynella quelchii* (Venezuela)	Philippe Kok
96	*Rhacophorus pardalis* (Borneo, Brunei)	Phil Bishop
98	*Rentapia rugosa* (Borneo, Sarawak)	Phil Bishop
100	*Scaphiophryne gottlebei* (Madagascar)	Gonçalo M. Rosa
102	*Rhacophorus dulitensis* (Borneo)	Ulmar Grafe
104	*Ranoidea aurea* (New Zealand)	Phil Bishop
106	*Hyperolius viridiflavus* (Africa)	Jos Kielgast
108	*Boophis elenae* (Madagascar)	Phil Bishop
110	*Excidobates mysteriosus* (Peru)	Jos Kielgast
112	*Microhyla borneensis* (Borneo, Sarawak)	Ulmar Grafe
114	*Phyllomedusa distincta* (Brazil)	Luis F. Marin da Fonte
116	*Leiopelma hochstetteri* (New Zealand)	Phil Bishop
118	*Polypedates* terrestrial tadpole (Sri Lanka)	James Reardon
120	*Boophis viridis* (Madagascar)	Gonçalo M. Rosa
122	*Espadarana prosoblepon* (Panama)	Gonçalo M. Rosa
124	*Hylarana raniceps* (Borneo, Brunei)	Phil Bishop
126	*Ranoidea chloris* (Australia)	Phil Bishop
128	*Bufo spinosus* (Morocco)	Debbie Bishop
130	*Guibemantis diphonus* (Madagascar)	Gonçalo M. Rosa
132	*Boophis jaegeri* (Madagascar)	Gonçalo M. Rosa
134	*Metaphrynella sundana* (Borneo)	Ulmar Grafe
136	*Rhacophorus rufipes* (Borneo, Brunei)	Phil Bishop
138	*Heterixalus punctatus* (Madagascar)	Phil Bishop
140	*Staurois latopalmatus* (Borneo, Brunei)	Phil Bishop
142	*Hyperolius veithi* (Congo Basin, Africa)	Jos Kielgast
144	*Itapotihyla langsdorffii* (Brazil)	Luis F. Marin da Fonte
146	*Mantella expectata* (Madagascar)	Gonçalo M. Rosa
148	*Ranoidea raniformis* (New Zealand)	Phil Bishop
150	*Hemiphractus proboscideus* (Brazil)	Jos Kielgast
152	*Staurois guttatus* (Borneo, Brunei)	Phil Bishop
154	*Rhinoderma darwinii* (Chile)	Phil Bishop
156	*Boana guentheri* (Argentina)	Phil Bishop
160	*Litoria infrafrenata* (Australia) and Debbie Bishop	Phil Bishop

Cover
Front cover: *Litoria infrafrenata* (Australia) Phil Bishop
Back cover, top row, far left: *Mantella expectata* (Madagascar) Gonçalo M. Rosa
Back cover, top row, 2ⁿᵈ from left *Megophrys nasuta* (Borneo, Brunei) Phil Bishop
Back cover, top row, 2ⁿᵈ from right: *Heterixalus madagascariensis* (Madagascar) Debbie Bishop
Back cover, top row, far right: *Dyscophus antongilii* (Madagascar) Phil Bishop
Back cover, bottom: *Limnonectes leporinus* (Borneo, Brunei) Phil Bishop
Spine: *Hylarana raniceps* (Borneo, Sarawak) Phil Bishop

Dedication

This book is dedicated to Debbie Bishop. Debbie was lucky enough to grow up in one of the best frog hot-spots (South Africa) and has accompanied me on many frog trips around the globe. She has worked tirelessly over the last 35 years as my field assistant and painstakingly takes photographs of every frog we encountered, despite being covered in mosquitos, up to her waist in crocodiles, and in the pouring rain. She is my soulmate, my confidante, my sense of reason, the mother of my children and my lovely wife.

First published 2021

Exisle Publishing Pty Ltd
226 High Street, Dunedin, 9016, New Zealand
PO Box 864, Chatswood, NSW 2057, Australia
www.exislepublishing.com

A CiP record for this book is available from the National Library of Australia.

ISBN 978 1 925820 81 2

Designed by Mark Thacker
Typeset in Archetype 24 on 36pt
Printed in China

This book uses paper sourced under ISO 14001 guidelines from well-managed forests and other controlled sources.

2 4 6 8 10 9 7 5 3 1